# Self Discipline

## *Unleash The Power Of Self Discipline, Influence And Willpower In Your Life To Achieve Anything*

By Ace McCloud
Copyright © 2014

# Disclaimer

The information provided in this book is designed to provide helpful information on the subjects discussed. This book is not meant to be used, nor should it be used, to diagnose or treat any medical condition. For diagnosis or treatment of any medical problem, consult your own physician. The publisher and author are not responsible for any specific health or allergy needs that may require medical supervision and are not liable for any damages or negative consequences from any treatment, action, application or preparation, to any person reading or following the information in this book. Any references included are provided for informational purposes only. Readers should be aware that any websites or links listed in this book may change.

# Table of Contents

DEDICATED TO THOSE WHO ARE PLAYING
THE GAME OF LIFE TO

WIN

KEEP ON PUSHING AND NEVER GIVE UP!

Ace McCloud

# Be sure to check out my website for all my Books and Audio books.

## www.AcesEbooks.com

# Introduction

I want to thank you and congratulate you for buying the book, "Self Discipline: Discover The True Power Of Discipline, Influence And Willpower"

This book contains proven steps and strategies on how to increase your self-discipline, your influence over others and how to strengthen your willpower so that you can maximize your success potential. Many of us know exactly what we should be doing, but aren't doing those things consistently. The goal of this book is to help you build up your inner reserves of strength so that you can do what needs to get done when it needs to get done! Some of the greatest people throughout history have had tremendous discipline and influence over others! If you want to make positive changes in your life and recreate your world the way you would like it to be, then you've chosen the right book!

# Chapter 1: How Discipline, Influence And Willpower Can Help You Succeed In Life

Influence, willpower and discipline are essential personal tools for success in any endeavor. However, most of us haven't developed these tools to their full potential.

Many people underestimate the power of these tools and fail to use them effectively. Influence and persuasion are needed on a daily basis, both in personal relationships and in the workplace. Mastering these skills may take a little time and effort, but once you do, you'll notice a whole variety of positive changes in your life. For instance, imagine being able to persuade and influence a friend or loved one to start eating healthier and to exercise. Or, think about the next time there is a promotion opportunity at work. The more influence you have, and the better your persuasion techniques are, the greater your chances are of securing that promotion and a large pay increase.

Willpower also plays a key role in your success throughout life. Being able to exert your will over a given situation increases your chances of success. We all know that willpower is needed to quit smoking or change our dietary habits, but few of us realize that we can increase the strength of our willpower and also increase the amount of willpower we have available to us. Without willpower, we achieve nothing, so these skills are massively important to utilize effectively.

Self-discipline works hand in hand with willpower. You need willpower to exert self-control, but you also need self-control to exert your willpower. That particular detail is discussed in more detail later in this book. When you learn how to control your negative urges, you will notice many more positive changes happening in your life, such as better finances, better job prospects, positive attitude changes, better relationships, and much more.

Combining all these skills together for peak performance will take time and practice, but for every positive change you make, you will notice that it becomes easier and easier. Over time, it will become second nature to you and form into a good habit that you will feel compelled to do every day. Once you get to that point, you will be able to redefine your world, focusing on what's important to you, and have much more success at bringing the things that give you true happiness into your life. Sitting here now, reading this book, you may feel like getting your life to be how you want it to be is an impossible dream. But don't be discouraged. The techniques we're about to look at are easy to implement in your life, and if used properly, you will very quickly start to notice some positive changes.

All the skills detailed in this book can help you to make targeted changes in various areas of your life. After you have mastered willpower, influence, and discipline, you will have the tools necessary to begin to reshape the world around you and achieve your desired goals.

So, what are you waiting for? Read on.

# Chapter 2: Influence and Persuasion

Influencing others and persuading those around you are two skills that you should master when trying to take control of your life. Some of the greatest leaders and people in history have had this ability, and they have been remembered throughout the centuries because of it.

There are different kinds of influence and persuasion techniques you can try to get the results you want. Don't forget, many of these techniques can be applied to yourself, as well as to others.

## Defining Influence

According to the Free Online Dictionary, influence can be defined as "a power affecting a person, thing, or course of events, especially one that operates without any direct or apparent effort: relaxed under the influence of the music; the influence of television on modern life", or the "power to sway or affect based on prestige, wealth, ability, or position: used her parent's influence to get the job."

In this day and age, influence is everywhere. It is in the television, radio, internet, billboards, magazines, newspapers, books, people, and much more. Everything we look at and everything we hear influences our decisions and the choices we make. With all these messages bombarding us at every turn, it's easy to forget that, we too, are capable of influencing the decision making of ourselves and others.

If we master the skill of influencing ourselves and others, it is only natural that the world will begin to reshape itself around us. It will begin to be full of more things that bring us joy and filled with fewer things that make us unhappy. So now that we know just how powerful influence can be, let's take a look at bringing more of it into our lives.

## Influence

The first technique we'll look at is how to make others feel valued by giving them recognition and involving them in decision making processes. Let's call this empowerment. Empowerment not only allows you to access other people's thought and opinions – what makes them tick – it also gives you the opportunity to discuss your way of thinking in an open and honest dialogue. When the decision is reached, the recognition that you give them for their involvement will make them more likely to reinforce your opinions the next time a decision comes up.

The second technique is to position your own ideas so that they meet the other persons concerns. The reason this is important is that it makes people feel valued. Once a person feels valued by you, they are much more open to other ideas, persuasion methods, or knowledge you may wish to utilize or share.

When relating this to yourself, you should take a look at your own concerns about the problem at hand so that you can do more research on them. Once you have done your research, you can eliminate any unfounded concerns you may have had, or use your new knowledge to implement a better strategy for accomplishing your desired goal. It is a good idea to write down all your concerns on a piece of paper, and then systematically go through them, taking notes as you go along. Once this is done, clearly write out the best strategy you can come up with to most effectively get the task or goal accomplished. It is also more compelling if you make this into a goal for yourself and set a deadline. Many famous people and peak performers have a written down list of goals for themselves and will read through them daily. Some will also visualize themselves accomplishing their goal over and over again in vivid detail in their mind to really increase their chances of goal accomplishment. It is also a good idea to make the goal seem easy when writing it down. For example, I will easily stop watching so much television and focus more of my time and energy on working out.

Another great influencing and persuasive technique involves bargaining with people, or with yourself. You can gain support from others by exchanging resources or favors. Think of this as a mutually rewarding experience. For example, if you like watching comedy movies and your partner likes action films, you can offer to reward your partner by saying that you'll watch two action movies with them next time if they let you watch that comedy film you've been dying to see right now.

In a business situation, you could offer to share some valuable information on an important subject in exchange for some other valuable information or service that would benefit you in your business or work environment. Bargaining is give and take. If you want to keep someone in your life as a valuable ally, then it will be important that they feel happy in their transactions with you. Similarly, if you are the one doing all the giving and the other person is only take, take, take, then this is a great time to find new friends. Building relationships with others involves listening to them and getting to know them. Maintaining solid and friendly communications with a new friend will let them know that you like them and are open to their ideas. Once they feel trusted and appreciated by you, then the majority of people will also be open to your ideas and ways of thinking. As you know, your reputation is vitally important in business and in life.

You can also apply bargaining to yourself. If you're trying desperately to lose weight, and are dreaming of eating some very unhealthy and high calorie food, then tell yourself that if you don't give in and instead eat some healthier foods for the next few days, then you will treat yourself to a nice massage at the end of the week.

Particularly in the world of business, one of the keys to persuasive success is to find out who the key influencers are in the workplace. Using some of the strategies we have already discussed, you can potentially put yourself in the position of influencing the influencers. This is great when it comes to promotions, as you can exert your influence upon the influencer to let them know just how much you want the promotion and how hard you would be willing to work once it was granted. A few good words from the influencer could be all that is needed to tip the scales in your favor. Once you have a degree of persuasive ability with an influencer, be sure to nourish this relationship, as it could pay huge dividends for you in a variety of other situations that pop up for you in the future.

By showing that you have a common vision and goals with those in the workplace or by those who you are in a relationship with is also a great way to strengthen a relationship. Sharing common visions with others is a powerful persuasive tool in its own right, but it also supplements other strategies such as relationship building. Common goals unite people, and the more united people feel with you, the more likely they will be to back up your ideas or to help you in a time of need.

Similar to sharing common visions and goals, look for things that you have in common that you can talk about. Maybe you both have kids, or both where athletes growing up. Maybe you both hate the cold weather or love a similar sports team. Maybe you both are animal lovers or are fitness enthusiasts. Go out of your way to find similarities and talk about them. Even if you don't like the same things, just showing that you care enough to find out what they enjoy is a great way to build friendship and trust. Be sure to do a lot of listening, another great skill for building a good relationship.

Another good way to persuade people is with logic. Present a person with an inalienable truth and they can't disagree with. Make sure you have your facts right, and the data to back it up, and you leave them with little room to argue.

Another incredible way to build rapport with people is to mirror them. This technique makes the other person feel that you are like they are. When this happens, it is much easier for that person to like you and trust you. For example, if someone likes to talk extremely loudly all the time, then talk back to them in a loud voice. If they are shy and talk very softly, talk very calmly and softly back to them. If their arms are crossed, you can casually cross your arms. If their legs are crossed, go ahead and cross your legs. If they like to smile a lot, smile right back at them. If they are very serious with a harsh tone, be serious right back to them with just as harsh a tone. Almost nobody is going to notice that you are mirroring them unless you take it too far. This is an incredible technique that will help you make friends and increase your influence.

So far, we've looked at positive strategies to persuade people. But some people choose to employ more negative persuasion techniques. We'll take a look at these now so that you can identify when these techniques are being used to try and persuade you.

Many people choose to persuade you by choosing the most dramatic way possible of presenting an idea. Crocodile tears, screaming, guilt trips, and temper tantrums are a few such ways. It's important to remember that when techniques such as these are being used against you, to maintain an emotional distance. Do not let yourself be drawn into a negative situation or influenced into making a hasty decision you will soon regret. When you give in to situations like these, it only reinforces the bad behavior, making it a tactic that person will more than likely use on you in future situations. You need to be strong and make the best decision for your own personal goals and dreams. When a negative behavior does not give the desired result, it will usually stop happening.

Some people also try to use coercion on you by pressuring you, reprimanding you, or threatening you. Don't let yourself fall into the trap of becoming afraid of people like this. Maintain an emotional distance from the situation and take time to think about how to deal with it in a positive and appropriate manner. In the heat of the moment in can be very easy to make less than ideal decisions!

**Persuasion**

So, now you know some great ways to influence people. But how do you persuade them if your influencing tactics haven't worked? Is it doable? You bet it is! People are doing it to you all the time.

Turn on the TV. Go ahead. Find a channel that's cut to a commercial break. Now watch one of the commercials. What did that commercial do? It tried to persuade you to buy that product, or donate to that charity, or something else advertisers wanted you to do. Did it work?

How did they persuade you or try to persuade you?

First of all, many commercials will focus on what's in it for you. They do this by demonstrating what may be missing from your life, or how your life would be greatly improved by their product. Perhaps there is a new dish detergent that moistens your skin instead of dehydrating it while you're washing the dishes, or maybe you've been shown how to keep your computer clean from viruses just by using their product.

More than likely, you'll be given examples of how their product has worked for thousands of people, just like you, or how nine out of ten doctors recommend this product over the competitors.

After they tell you all of the different ways the product can benefit you, then you will usually be bombarded with facts, testimonials, and figures to back up their claims.

Finally, don't forget that this particular offer is limited to the first one hundred callers or only for customers who buy now. In essence, you'll have been shown that the product is in short supply, so you must hurry. This technique makes the product seem more valuable than it actually is because of the scarcity of it.

So let's list those steps and discuss how you can use each one to persuade other people. We'll do this by supposing that Janet wants to persuade her husband Jack to buy a new car, while Jack, is reluctant to take out another loan to cover the cost of a new vehicle. He believes that their current vehicles are just fine.

1. Focus on what's in it for them. Make sure they know what is missing from their lives, or how their lives will be drastically improved.

   Janet starts out by telling Jack that the new car comes with a 100,000 mile warranty, and that all repair costs are covered by the manufacturer, not just labor. She continues by telling Jack that he wouldn't need to spend so much time on the weekends performing maintenance and fixing the car because scheduled servicing is also included. She finishes by telling Jack that they could spend more time together doing the things that they enjoy rather than her watching him underneath the car all weekend.

2. Give examples of how it has worked for others in the past.

   Janet tells Jack that George and Mildred next door bought a new car and it has saved them thousands in gas mileage and servicing costs, and that Mildred said it drives like a dream, even in the snow, which, she tells Jack, is something that she has been concerned about for a while now.

3. Back up the product or idea with facts and figures.

   Before presenting her idea to Jack, Janet has done a bit of homework and found that the insurance on the new car is hundreds of dollars cheaper per year than on her old one. Not only that, but by the time you calculate in servicing costs, gas mileage costs, and annual repair bills, it would actually save them some money over the course of the next several years. Also, the local dealership is offering low cost financing that would decrease costs further.

4. Make sure they know that this product or offer is limited, thus increasing its perceived value.

   Janet lets Jack know that the low cost financing deal is only running until the end of the week, and that after that, the finance cost will be nearly double what the dealership is offering right now. Also, if they use Janet's old car as a trade in, the dealership is offering a three-thousand dollar instant rebate along with a hefty discount off the car's sticker price.

Knowing that Jack's a huge football fan, she says that with that kind of cash they could afford a two week vacation right around the time of the Superbowl!

Poor Jack really didn't stand a chance, did he? Although this example is a bit stereotypical, and completely fictional, it does show the steps of persuasion in action.

# Chapter 3: Willpower

The American Psychological Association defines willpower as "the ability to resist short-term temptations in order to meet long-term goals." Many people consider their lack of willpower to be the number one reason why they fail at such things such as learning new skills, quitting smoking, and losing weight, among other things. When we feel that we have a lack of willpower, we feel like we are 'weak' individuals, and use this weakness to talk ourselves out of putting in the work necessary to accomplish our goals. Once you have gotten in the habit of quitting and giving up, it gets easier and easier to put things off and make excuses instead of doing what really needs to get done. The main thing that separates winners from losers is that winners have a strong willpower and they don't give up, even if they fail, and keep at it until they are successful.

There have been several studies designed to find out whether willpower is a resource that different people have at different levels, and whether this precious resource is only available to us in limited amounts. You may be surprised to learn that these studies did indeed find that willpower is a limited resource: We only have so much of it to spend on accomplishing our given goals. Once this resource is depleted, we are almost certain to fail in accomplishing our desired goal.

Let's continue with the idea that willpower is a limited resource. Like any resource, it can be depleted and restored. Think of it like planting two trees every time you cut one down, or going to the gas station to fill up your car when the fuel tank is low. If we think about willpower in these terms, then it is possible for us to do certain things that will help restore low levels of willpower and to also do certain things to ensure our willpower remains strong over long periods of time. After all, if we plant two trees for every one we cut down, we are increasing our resource pool. Likewise, we can fill up emergency gas containers to store in our car and use them if the need should arise.

**Fuelling your Willpower**

Studies have shown that people who have low blood glucose levels have less reserves of willpower than people with typical levels of glucose in their bloodstream. While this is important in fuelling your willpower levels, it is equally important not to allow your blood glucose levels to become too high. High blood glucose levels have been linked to obesity, heart disease, pre-diabetes, and diabetes. So, what are the best ways of maintaining a healthy blood glucose level?

The first thing to do is cut down on sugary snacks and beverages. And yes, you're right: This will take willpower. However, the small expenditure of willpower you spend on resisting the sugary snack is nothing compared to how much willpower you'll build as your body rids itself of all that refined sugar and empty calories and carbohydrates. You'll also notice that your energy levels improve as your body becomes less dependent on refined sugars and caffeine for boosting your energy levels throughout the day. Your energy will become more stable as opposed to the energy bursts and crashes that comes with consuming sugary foods and drinks. With increased energy, it becomes much easier to exert your willpower effectively.

Another great way of maintaining a healthy blood glucose level is to always choose a wholegrain option when it is available to you. Most grocery stores carry wholegrain versions of breads, pastas, rice, and cereals. This should be an easy switch for anyone. Quite simply, wholegrain foods taste better than their refined counterparts, and will leave you feeling fuller for longer. It is also easier for you to resist snacking on sugary snacks throughout the day when you are not hungry. A quick final note: Check the labels on cereals that advertise themselves as wholegrain. While it is great to have wholegrain cereal, many of these products have huge amounts of refined sugar in them.

Massively important in the effort to rebuild and increase your resource pool of willpower is eating a good dose of fruits and vegetables. Try choosing to eat an apple over that high sugar candy bar. The energy you get from apples will last longer than the energy from a candy bar, and you won't experience a sugar crash after the initial burst of energy that the sugar gives you. You can also try eating oranges instead of drinking orange juice. They're lower in calories, help fight hunger, and give you an energy boost, all at the same time they're delivering vital vitamins and minerals into your body.

The more energy you have has a direct impact on the levels of willpower you are able to access. As we've seen, diet is an important factor in this. But, did you know that regular exercise also builds up your energy levels? Simple changes in your daily routine can increase your energy levels exponentially. Walking is one of the best exercises. It is very low impact but has most of the benefits of running. Try and take a walk every day, or just try taking the stairs or parking in a spot further away. These things don't require a massive amount of willpower to perform, and you don't have to join a gym or spend large amounts of money. All you have to do is keep yourself as active as possible, which, with the changes in your diet, should leave you with plenty of energy to exert your willpower when it is needed most.

Perhaps the most vital thing to remember in keeping a healthy blood glucose level and, therefore, increasing the amount of willpower you have available to draw upon, is to keep a healthy weight. If you are overweight or underweight, you are detrimentally impacting the amount of willpower you will have available. Find a healthy diet and exercise routine that works for you. It is no surprise that many of the most successful people in the world are healthy, strong, and fit. They put in the effort to maintain their body at peak levels so that they will have the energy and willpower needed to get their goals accomplished. For some serious information on how to do this like a pro, check out my book: Anti-aging Cure.

Once you are in shape and exercising regularly, it will become a healthy habit, and it is much easier to stay in shape than it is to get in shape.

## Mood and Willpower

Good mood has been shown to have a direct influence on our levels of willpower. Being in a positive mood gives us more energy and inspiration to accomplish our goals that require willpower. Let's think about this for a moment. If we are feeling good after watching a life-affirming movie, for instance, we are much more likely to make some positive choices in our actions for the next few days. It's similar to the effect that can be gained from attending a twelve-step recovery meeting: You leave the meeting with a positive mindset (recovery is possible) and with the goal to make more positive choices (I don't need that drink/drugs/etc. to be happy).

So how do we recreate positive feelings in our day-to-day lives?

Having a positive self-image goes a long way in enabling us to build up increasingly higher levels of willpower. As we are bombarded every day by images of supermodels and beautiful people, we need to be realistic about our body image. We can strive for greatness, but don't get too overly concerned about it to the extent that it will limit your success potential. There are millions of success stories about average looking people going on to achieve incredible things. Many people who may not be athletic or the best looking use this as fuel to work even that much harder than everyone else to ensure their success.

Self-acceptance is a great way to build that positive self-image. We're not perfect. Get over it. We all have our flaws, and we all have things that we're good at. What's important is that we are making a good strategic plan and doing our best to accomplish it as effectively as possible, helping ourselves and other people along the way. Take every opportunity to give yourself credit for all the hard work and great things that you have done in your life. Keeping a diary is also a good idea. Be sure to write down or voice record the good things that happen in your life, it is always fun to sit down and read them or hear them back years later when you may be feeling down.

## Here is a great exercise designed to help you in having a solid foundation for your self-esteem.

Take a piece of paper and divide it into two sections and call them 'positives' and 'negatives'. Write down in each column all of the things you feel are positive about in your life and all the things that you consider to be negative in your life. Now, ask a close friend or your partner to do the same about you and then add all the results together. Take all of the negative things and then do some research to get an idea of how you can improve upon them. Then, take all the positives in your life and put them all together on a separate list that you can look over when needed or daily to help get yourself in a more resourceful frame of mind.

You may be pleasantly surprised by what other people may think about you and this will help you to build a more positive self-image. Once your self-image is rock solid, it will become a valuable ally for you in your travels through life. You will also find it much easier to feel more positive about your life, and your future success potential. Put all this together, and it will increase your levels of willpower tremendously. You may even discover willpower reserves that you didn't even know you had!

So, how else can we maintain a good mood? It's not just about how you feel about yourself; good mood can be attained from your surroundings as well. And no, it doesn't mean you have to live on the sunny island of Hawaii, or have a mansion in the middle of the forest.

Whether you live in a tiny apartment in the middle of a big city or a detached five bedroom log cabin overlooking the Connecticut River, it is important that you are happy there. If you're not happy, make a change. It's imperative.

If you are happy where you live, but you just don't feel happy, try taking stock of the conditions you're living in. Go through your house or apartment and write down a list of all the things you don't like. Perhaps there are pictures you don't like, or maybe you don't like the color of the walls. Is the room too cluttered? Does it need a serious clean? Is the furniture looking old and shabby? Could it use some plants? Whatever you are unhappy with, make sure you write it all down. Also, be sure to write down any ideas you have to make the area more to your liking.

Next, prioritize. What can you do right away? What costs money? What can you do for free? What is the most annoying thing you would like to fix? Be sure to write down your priorities realistically. There's no point putting 'Replace Sofa' as your number one priority when you know that you can't afford it at the moment.

De-cluttering and cleaning your living space will give you an instant boost of wellbeing. It is also a great opportunity to make some extra money by selling all those things you haven't used in several years and that are only taking up valuable space. Also, repainting shabby walls will give a new lease of life to your home. Try to choose colors that make you feel happy. Warmer colors such as beiges, yellows, and oranges often have a more positive impact on mood than colder colors such as blues and greens. But, choose whatever colors make you feel happy; don't worry about what anybody else may think, they don't live there!

Finally, an incredible way to bring laughter and joy into your life is to actively pursue it. My mood brightening book: Laughter Therapy goes into serious detail on how to improve your life with laughter among other things. The book includes laughter yoga, mood enhancing foods, and many other all natural and time tested methods to help make your life more fulfilling and filled with joy and happiness.

## Exercising your Willpower

Willpower can also be thought of as like any other muscle in your body: If you work at it often enough, it will get stronger and more flexible. Exercising your willpower regularly is enough to make it stronger and more durable. If you think back to having willpower as a limited resource, which you want to have more of, using your willpower regularly will help 'deepen' this precious resource.

In modern culture, there is very little we have to wait for any more to gain gratification. With all the on-demand services available, food delivery services, grocery delivery, express postal services, instant downloads, movies on demand, etc., gratification is, in many cases, just a few clicks away. But, not all that long ago, we had to wait for things. Waiting built up anticipation and appreciation. It is important to think of gratification as being better when it is delayed.

Delayed gratification can build the strength of your willpower and the amount of it you have available in reserve. So, a good way of exercising your willpower is to delay your gratification. Try this: The next time you decide you want the latest must have gadget, wait. Don't buy it right away. The longer you can fight the urge to buy it, the harder you're working your willpower and building its strength. If you delay your purchase long enough, not only will you have exercised your willpower, you may have found something else much better to spend your money on.

There is a famous study of a scientist who took a bunch of children and offered them a treat. The children were told that if they could wait fifteen minutes without eating the treat, then they would be given an additional treat. Many years later, the scientist caught up with these children, and what he concluded was that those children who were able to show some willpower and not eat the treat initially, and therefore get two treats after waiting, where far more successful later in life than those children who ate the initial treat immediately.

Therefore, it would be wise to try and not to make rash or hasty decisions. Go ahead and build up your willpower by waiting and spending your time wisely researching your best course of action.

## How to Use your Willpower

Once you have strengthened your willpower, and increased the amount of it you have available, you're going to want to use it effectively. Read through the tips below and begin to incorporate these habits into your life one at a time.

- Make a weekly or monthly plan about how you will achieve your goals. Setting a plan like this allows you to adjust should things not go your way immediately. Make your goals seem easy to accomplish when writing them down.

- Be optimistic about the future and what life holds for you. Being pessimistic about things can almost become a self-fulfilling prophecy. Do your best to focus on positive things and try to be grateful for all the good things in your life. Make a list of things you are grateful for and review it often. Also, be sure to go through your goals and self-affirming positive attributes on a daily basis to build a strong sense of self confidence. If you find negative thoughts and feelings are intruding too much into your daily life, a great resource that I have found on YouTube that can be used to help reduce or eliminate some of the effects of negative thoughts and memories are: Eliminating Procrastination - Self Talk with WHEE Tapping and Eliminating Self-Sabotage - Self-Talk with WHEE Tapping both by PositiveSelfTalk.

- Be clear about your thoughts and opinions. Confidence is key to maximizing your willpowers full potential. Negative feelings and thoughts can be a real drain on your willpower reserves.

- Raise your standards. Things go along much more smoothly when you are doing them like a pro. This will be a serious test for your willpower, but if you want to truly reach your potential, your standards will have to be raised.

- Be sure and get enough sleep. It may be beneficial at some points to neglect your sleep to pull an all nighter, but over the long term, this is a strategy that does not work very well. There are hundreds of studies showing the benefits of sleep. I know that I personally do by far my best work when I am fully rested and highly alert.

- A great collection of beautiful pictures or a book of inspiring quotes can be a great way to help build up your willpower reserves. A great habit to have every day is to spend ten minutes reading through uplifting quotes or looking at beautiful and awe inspiring pictures.

- One of my favorite things to do when I was growing up was to video tape myself winning or playing a hot new video game. This was especially fun when I was a Pro gamer and had utterly mastered the games. Later on, I would take my favorite scenes from over the years and edit them into an action packed movie thriller of my greatest accomplishments in the video game realms. Now, whenever I need a recharge, I can just sit back and watch all these incredible video game victories. It's a great way that I have found to re-charge my willpower. By the way, you are only allowed to do this for personal use.

- Make a list of all the great things you have done in your life. All the incredible relationships you've had. All the goals you have been able to accomplish. All the fun trips you have been on. All of your favorite memories. All of your grand victories. You would be surprised at how easy it can be to forget about these over time. Be sure to write them all down and then go over them whenever you need a willpower super charge.

- Tackle one large goal at a time rather than multiple small ones. It is much easier to truly be effective by focusing all your intention on one thing at a time! Be sure to categorize what needs to get done in the order of priority, and then focus like a laser on each individual task until it is accomplished.

- Reaffirm your goals to yourself every day. Affirmation of your goals and recognizing your own achievements will keep your willpower firm and unwavering. You will become more determined to keep at it. Also, be sure to reward yourself for your achievements. Visualize your goals as if they have already been accomplished.

- Help other people to achieve their goals. By helping others, you will demonstrate the positive changes you have made and you will see the positive effects that your techniques have on others.

- Success is the only option. With a mindset like that, you are focusing your willpower on one objective only. No longer are you giving yourself, or your willpower, the opportunity to fail. A famous quote from Thomas A. Edison, one of the greatest inventors of all time is: "I have not failed. I've just found ten thousand ways that won't work."

# Chapter 4: Discipline

So, in the last chapter, we talked about willpower and how to increase the strength of your willpower and how do increase the quantity of willpower you have available. Some of the ways to build your willpower will require some self-discipline. Conversely, your ability to discipline yourself requires willpower. It's easy to see that discipline and willpower are very closely related things. But whether you choose to start working your discipline or willpower, you're going to need to exert some self-control.

## Building your Self-Discipline

Like in the willpower exercise we discussed in the previous chapter, it is important to begin change with a look at ourselves. Divide a page in half and write down 'Strengths/Goals' at the top of one half, and write down 'Changes that need to be made/weaknesses to work on' at the top of the other. A strength/goal might include 'Enjoy the outdoors more often', and a change that needs to be made/weaknesses might be 'I don't get enough exercise'.

Using the example above, it is quite easy to see that some positive changes can be made using only one adjustment in your life. All you would need to do is make it a priority to take a walk outdoors every once in a while. However, if your list is long, which many people's lists are, it's important not to feel overwhelmed and, therefore, it's important to remember to just make one change at a time.

Making one change at a time requires less willpower than making many changes at once. Also, making too many changes at the same time can be confusing and overwhelming, and being overwhelmed increases your chances of failure and becoming demotivated. Like mentioned earlier in the book, it is far better to put all your focus on accomplishing the most important task at hand than it is to spread your focus in many different directions.

Here's something to think about. If you have a pile of sand, a pile of large rocks, and an empty container, and it's your job to fit everything into that container, what do you put into the container first? The rocks or the sand? While you may think it's going to be easier to get the sand in first, and then put the rocks on top, you'll find that the large rocks no longer fit. If you put all the large rocks in first, and then pour the sand over the top, the sand will settle between the rocks enabling you to fit everything in. Thought about in those terms, it's important to tackle the major changes first, and you may just find that all the little things take care of themselves.

Now go ahead and take a look at your list and use that as a guide to see what possible changes you could make that would make your life more successful or enjoyable. Try and be strategic. Tackle the bigger things first. But to tackle the bigger things you are going to need a good dose of willpower and motivation. So take that big thing in your life that you want to change and circle it on your list.

Now make a new list, and explain in great detail how this change will benefit your life and the positive things that would happen in your life if you were to accomplish this goal. Think of all the benefits you will gain, or how it will benefit the people around you. These benefits may be financial, emotional, or any number of other things. Each time you write down a reason, chances are you will have become more motivated to make that change in your life. This is a list you can look at every day to keep yourself motivated, so don't just use it once and then forget about it. Keep it fresh in your mind until it is accomplished. When you are relaxing, just close your eyes and visualize yourself accomplishing the goal. Make this visualization enjoyable and compelling; this will greatly increase your chances of accomplishing the goal if done often enough and with enough intensity.

It is always a good idea to plan things out. If your big goal is to quit smoking, how will you cope with the changes and urges you will experience during the quitting process? If you're planning on losing weight, think about when your willpower will be tested. Will it be at lunch time with a convenient fast-food restaurant? Maybe you will be tested at a birthday celebration? How will you cope with all the delicious but extremely unhealthy food? The more planning you do, the greater your chances are of success. Be sure to try and devise plans and strategies that utilize your natural strengths and tendencies as much as possible.

Don't worry if you take a step backward. It is common to be unable to resist temptation or immediate gratification sometimes. After all, we are only human. But it's important to recognize that you haven't failed. All you need to do is reflect on why you took that little step backwards and then make appropriate plan changes for future occurrences in similar situations. Think about if you could turn back time, how would you do it differently?

In addition to recognizing places where you went off track a little bit, you must also learn to recognize when you have done well. After a week or so, try thinking about all the things you have done right in making your changes successful. Think about all you struggled with, and what you didn't struggle with at all.

Most importantly, reward yourself for your successes. Give yourself a pat on the back and do something or buy something nice for yourself.

**Discipline with your health**

One of the areas many of us don't discipline ourselves enough in is our health. All too often we neglect ourselves in favor of work commitments, or obligations to our family and friends. Due to modern, busy lifestyles, we often forget to take the time necessary to properly look after ourselves.

We've already discussed the importance of a healthy diet and its impact on both willpower and our ability to exert self-discipline. But just as important as diet is sleep and reflection time. A sleep deficit, where we have not had enough rest and sleep to operate at peak efficiency, affects our energy levels as well as our ability to think and to concentrate. When we get enough sleep it is much easier to maintain self-discipline.

Time to relax and reflect is also important. A calm, clear mind allows us to consider events and how to approach them 'with your ultimate success and goals in mind'. The importance of having this valuable time cannot be stressed enough. Try and make the time to take a nap, meditate, or listen to a guided meditation on a subject you may be interested in improving upon. One of my favorite places to get guided meditations is at Hypnosis Downloads.

## Discipline with money

Money is another area in which self-discipline is of paramount importance. It's all too easy to buy whatever we want, whenever we want, particularly in the internet based, instant gratification age.

When taking control of your life, you must be in control of your finances. Take time to think about whether the item you are thinking about purchasing is something that you really need, or if it is simply something you want. Then, be sure to do some research to make sure that you are getting exactly what you need at a good price. Be wary of trying to save some money on cheap items, it can end up costing you later on. I have found it is usually better to spend a little more on a quality item that will last longer and that will make you happy, than on something that is cheap and on sale only for it to break or be outdated soon after. Also, find areas in your life where you can save money. You can eat much healthier and for far less money if you cook healthy at home rather than spending large amounts of money going out or ordering out for less healthy food.

It's also a good idea to make a list of all the money you have coming in and all money you are spending. Whatever money have left over that is not being used on essentials, exercise some self-discipline and willpower to save it up for more intelligent purchases in the future or to pay down existing debt.

Debt problems can quickly escalate, so it's important that you acknowledge to yourself if you are experiencing difficulties, and seek help if needed.

Remember this: Take care of the cents, and the dollars will take care of themselves.

## Discipline with harmful substances

Many people smoke cigarettes, or other substances, and drink alcoholic beverages on a regular basis. It's important to take control of how much of these products (if any) that you consume for a few reasons.

First, all of them are harmful to your health. We've just discussed the importance of looking after ourselves on the road to taking control of our lives, and substances that are considered to be minor poisons to the body certainly are not going to help you.

Second, they are all expensive. Again, we've just discussed the importance of taking control of your finances, so use some self-discipline and willpower and spend your hard earned money on life boosting healthier products that instead of destroying your motivation and your body, help you to stay motivated and live healthier.

Finally, harmful substances affect your brain and its ability to be in control and to think clearly. Try to remember the last time you had a completely logical discussion, where you were completely in control of your thoughts, when you were wasted drunk. If you can, you might want to ask the person you were talking to how you sounded. It probably wasn't as logical and in control as you remember it.

## Time Management

Try and be disciplined about your time management. Things get easier and easier if you make it a habit to stick to a regular schedule. The greatest individuals and organizations in the world all know how to manage time effectively. Throughout the day your time should be optimized for your own peak performance. Once you have determined what the best times are for you to eat, exercise, play, work, strategize, re-energize, rest, etc. then you need to be disciplined and do these things when they need to get done. Time management is an incredible skill to have and is valued by almost everyone. No one enjoys having their time wasted waiting on someone else. If you can be counted upon to be punctual, prepared, and reliable, then you are much more valuable not only to those around you, but to yourself as well. Having the discipline to manage your time effectively will be one of the best things you can do to increase your success potential.

# Chapter 5: Great Role Models

So what can willpower, influence, and self-discipline do for you? In addition to the things we have discussed in the book so far, it's important to realize that utilizing these skills in your day-today life will enable you to make huge life changes in whatever you put your mind to.

Using willpower, influence, and self-discipline, there are a massive number of people who have made a global impact with their lives. These are not only qualities that they used on a day-to-day basis; they use these abilities to change the world we live in.

In this chapter, we're going to take a look at some famous figures from throughout history that have used their influence, willpower, and self-discipline to get the results they wanted out of their lives. As you're reading about these giants among men, try to imagine yourself in their shoes, and think about the things you can do to make your life and the world a better place.

### John D. Rockefeller
"I do not think that there is any other quality so essential to success of any kind as the quality of perseverance. It overcomes almost everything, even nature." – John D. Rockefeller

Growing up, John D. Rockefeller had little guidance from his father who was a traveling salesman. His first job was as a bookkeeper, but he used his willpower to save up all his money to buy some oil refineries. These became a company known as Standard Oil.

By exerting his influence and willpower over his investments and businesses to increase their efficiency, Rockefeller became the richest man in the world at the time, and a legendary success.

### Ralph Lauren
"Knowledge is not a passion from without the mind, but an active exertion of the inward strength, vigor, and power of the mind, displaying itself from within." – Ralph Lauren

Ralph Lauren's upbringing was a world away from the polo games and country clubs that have inspired his clothing designs. In fact, his family was poor immigrants from Belarus, and he grew up sharing a bedroom with two brothers. At school, he used to make ties to sell to his friends. The proceeds from his sales, he invested in expensive suits.

Although several design houses turned down Ralph Lauren's tie designs, he persevered and used his growing influence to finally release a range of 'Polo' ties. The rest, as they say, is history.

## Frederick Douglass

"Allowing only ordinary ability and opportunity, we may explain success mainly by one word and that word is WORK! WORK!! WORK!!! WORK!!!!" – Frederick Douglass

Frederick Douglass was a slave whose master's wife began teaching him to read. When he was reprimanded by his master, he began learning from their children instead. He was traded to another master, who beat Douglass and whipped him. One day Douglass decided to confront his master and persuaded him to stop beating him, which he did.

In 1838, Douglass escaped from slavery to Massachusetts where he became an abolitionist, public speaker, author, and publisher.

Willpower, self-discipline, and influence were all skills Douglass relied upon throughout his life. Without them, he would have died a slave.

## Thomas Edison

"It is astonishing what an effort it seems to be for many people to put their brains definitely and systematically to work." –Thomas Edison

Edison only had a few months of formal schooling – they kicked him out for being too easily distracted. He was homeschooled for most of his life by his mother. After he saved a stationmaster's son from being hit by a train, he was offered a job as a telegraph operator. Edison offered to work nights so that he could tinker with the machinery and experiment.

Persistence and willpower paid off, and he created many inventions over time including the first commercially available incandescent light bulb. He eventually created General Electric and patented over one-thousand five-hundred inventions in his lifetime.

Making the choice to continue doing what he loved to do is what rescued Edison from a life of mediocrity as a telegraph operator.

## Arnold Schwarzenegger

"For me life is continuously being hungry. The meaning of life is not simply to exist, to survive, but to move ahead, to go up, to achieve, to conquer." – Arnold Schwarzenegger.

Before Arnold Schwarzenegger became a famous actor and governor of California, he had a very difficult upbringing. His family was poor and his father was distant and abusive. Very early on, Arnold decided he was going to leave home in search of a better future.

He starting bodybuilding in his mid-teens and studied psychology to sharpen his mind and build his willpower. After becoming Mr. Universe at the age of 20, he moved to America and won six more Mr. Olympia bodybuilding titles, putting him as one of the greatest, if not the greatest bodybuilder of all time.

Due to his thick Austrian accent, and his massive body, it took many years and much persistence for him to land his first acting roles. He got his big break in Conan the Barbarian, which was a massive success. He then went on to be one of the highest paid actors in the world for nearly twenty years straight. From there, Arnold turned his willpower and influence to politics and ran to become the governor of California: a race that he won.

Take a look at this YouTube documentary about Arnold Schwarzenegger and his rise from mediocrity: Arnold Schwarzenegger's Amazing Motivational Story posted by StormJB1. Another great YouTube video is Arnold's six secrets to success: Six Secrets To Success - Official posted by Travis Fisher.


**Tony Robbins**
"A real decision is measured by the fact that you've taken a new action. If there's no action, you haven't truly decided." – Tony Robbins

Tony Robbins is one of the most successful public speakers ever to have lived. Not only did he use his willpower, self-discipline, and persuasion to get where he is today, he continues to use these skills to help millions of people around the world. Below are some of his key philosophies and teachings.

- You can control your emotions by controlling your body language, breathing, language and focus.
- You can control your associations about pleasure and pain to greatly increase your success potential.
- To be successful you must fully commit to change.
- You can break the patterns of self-destructive behaviors by interrupting your typical daily routine.
- Making decisions is the ultimate power you hold. Deciding to change is the best weapon you have.
- We are shaped by our physical and emotional state. Both of which can be controlled and changed.
- **Happiness can be achieved by fulfilling six, basic human needs: Certainty, variety, connection with others, significance, growth and contribution.**
- Everything happens for a reason.
- Take responsibility for all of your actions.
- Learn from others who are successful.
- Success cannot be achieved without your full commitment.

For a great motivational message from Tony, check out this YouTube video: Tony Robbins Video On Keys To Massive Success by Ron Henley. Some other great videos from Tony: <u>Tony Robbins on Focus</u> posted by OwnYourReality and <u>Tony Robbins on the difference between a Winner and a Loser</u> posted by Refpeople – Social Network.

# Conclusion

I hope this book was able to help you to increase your influence over yourself and other people! I also hope that you have learned how to increase your willpower and how to build up substantial reserves of it. Finally, I hope you now know exactly how to utilize self-discipline effectively in your life.

The next step is to utilize the methods we have talked about in this book, and implement them into your life. Don't try to do too much at one time and be sure to keep a record of your progress that accurately reflects the successes that you are having. And, of course, don't forget to reward yourself when that goal is accomplished!

Finally, if you discovered at least one thing that has helped you or that you think would be beneficial to someone else, be sure to take a few seconds to easily post a quick positive review. As an author, your positive feedback is desperately needed. Your highly valuable five star reviews are like a river of golden joy flowing through a sunny forest of mighty trees and beautiful flowers! *To do your good deed in making the world a better place by helping others with your valuable insight, just leave a nice review.*

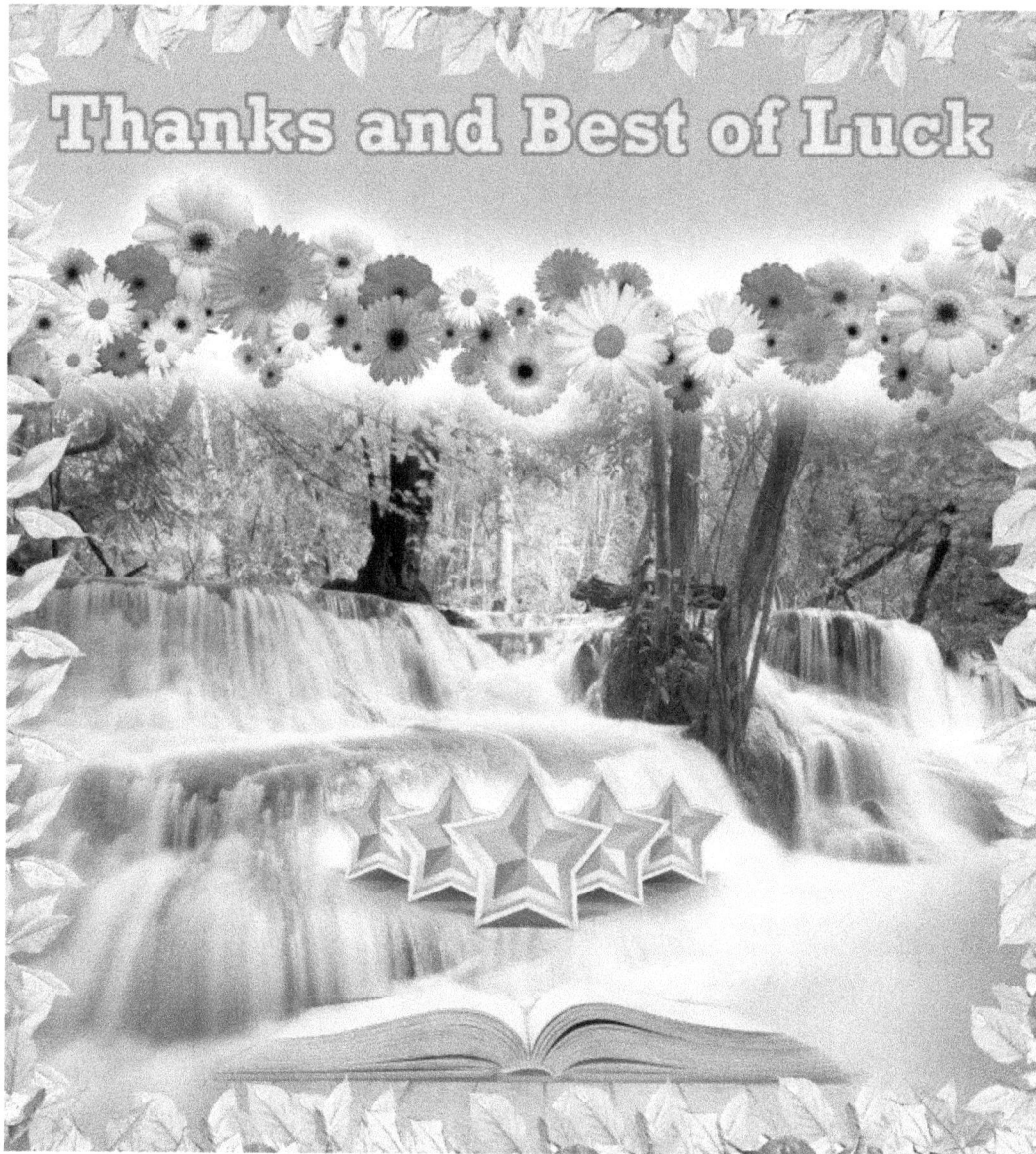
Thanks and Best of Luck

**My Other Books and Audio Books**
www.AcesEbooks.com

# Peak Performance Books

# Health Books

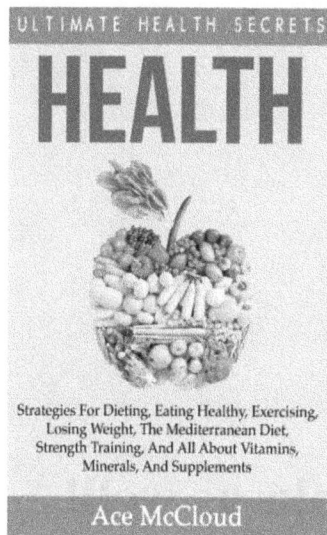

ULTIMATE HEALTH SECRETS

**HEALTH**

Strategies For Dieting, Eating Healthy, Exercising,
Losing Weight, The Mediterranean Diet,
Strength Training, And All About Vitamins,
Minerals, And Supplements

Ace McCloud

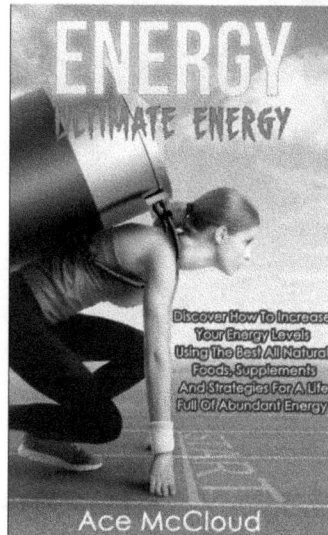

**ENERGY**
ULTIMATE ENERGY

Discover How To Increase
Your Energy Levels
Using The Best All Natural
Foods, Supplements
And Strategies For A Life
Full Of Abundant Energy

Ace McCloud

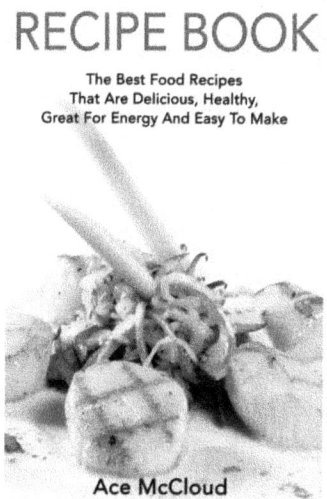

RECIPE BOOK

The Best Food Recipes
That Are Delicious, Healthy,
Great For Energy And Easy To Make

Ace McCloud

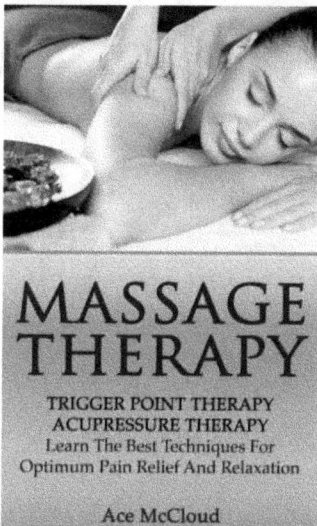

**MASSAGE THERAPY**

TRIGGER POINT THERAPY
ACUPRESSURE THERAPY
Learn The Best Techniques For
Optimum Pain Relief And Relaxation

Ace McCloud

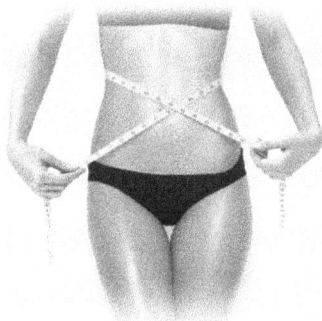

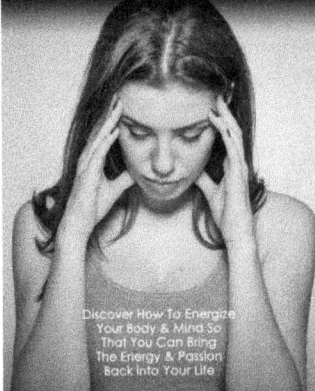

# Be sure to check out my audio books as well!

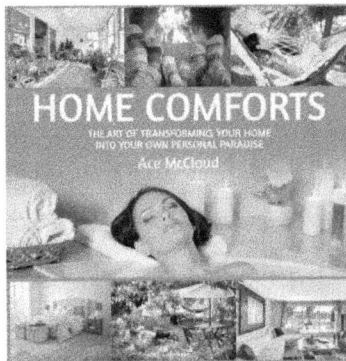

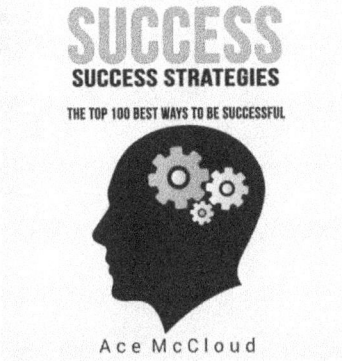

Check out my website at: www.AcesEbooks.com for a complete list of all of my books and high quality audio books. I enjoy bringing you the best knowledge in the world and wish you the best in using this information to make your journey through life better and more enjoyable! **Best of luck to you!**